Mason

May your dream become
a reality!

[signature]

Read + Prosper!
All THE BEST,
[signature]
James

99 Questions
to ask **BEFORE** starting a business in the US

RENATA CASTRO, ESQ.,
JAMES CHITTENDEN

BALBOA.PRESS
A DIVISION OF HAY HOUSE

Copyright © 2021 Renata Castro, Esq., James Chittenden.

All rights reserved. No part of this book may be used or reproduced by any means, graphic, electronic, or mechanical, including photocopying, recording, taping or by any information storage retrieval system without the written permission of the author except in the case of brief quotations embodied in critical articles and reviews.

Balboa Press books may be ordered through booksellers or by contacting:

Balboa Press
A Division of Hay House
1663 Liberty Drive
Bloomington, IN 47403
www.balboapress.com
844-682-1282

Because of the dynamic nature of the Internet, any web addresses or links contained in this book may have changed since publication and may no longer be valid. The views expressed in this work are solely those of the author and do not necessarily reflect the views of the publisher, and the publisher hereby disclaims any responsibility for them.

This book does not establish an attorney/client relationship. It is not a substitute for a consultation with an attorney. This book is for educational and entertainment purposes and does not constitute legal advice.

Any people depicted in stock imagery provided by Getty Images are models, and such images are being used for illustrative purposes only. Certain stock imagery © Getty Images.

Print information available on the last page.

ISBN: 978-1-9822-7917-2 (sc)
ISBN: 978-1-9822-7918-9 (e)

Balboa Press rev. date: 02/17/2022

CONTENTS

Authors' Notes ix
Acknowledgements xi
Foreword xiii
Praise for 99 Questions to ask BEFORE
starting a business in the US xv
Introduction xvii

Chapter 1   Why 99 Questions? 1
Chapter 2   How to Best Use This Book 3
Chapter 3   Glossary of Investment-Related Visas 5
Chapter 4   THE 99 Questions 15
Chapter 5   You have the answers. What now? 115

Recommended Reading List 119
About the Authors 121
About the Editor 123

GET A COPY OF 'PUBLIC TRIUMPH' FOR FREE!

READ THIS FIRST

"Marketing is key to your business success, so we are giving you a FREE copy of Public Triumph to give you more tools to successfully market your business."
— *James and Renata*

Go to **www.oneclickadvisor.com/book** to get your FREE copy now.

AUTHORS' NOTES

Renata Castro– Visit our website www.castrolegalgroup.com for information on immigration options from A to Z, including those for entrepreneurs and investors. Also make sure to follow our Instagram page @immigratetotheusa.

James Chittenden- If you are considering starting a business or have recently started a business, check out www.oneclickadvisor.com, where you can use the One Click Advisor Business Builder to make rapid progress on creating the business of your dreams.

ACKNOWLEDGEMENTS

Renata

To my children, Lucas, and Sofia, who taught me obstinance beyond belief, because once I became a mom, failure was not an option.

To my mother, uncle, and sister, who tolerated more than 99 questions I have asked on a daily basis, since 1982.

To Mike Castro, who handles forks on the road majestically.

To James, for the intellectual stimulation only good questions can bring.

To America, the land of the free and the home of the brave.

James

To thousands of business owners and would-be business owners who personally came to me for help, whether at the bank or looking for education or consulting. I learned from you, just as you learned from me. We leveled up together with great results. This book is one of them.

You might know someone fluent in multiple languages and cultures. You might know someone who is fluent in the law. You might know someone who is fluent in business. And you might know someone who is fluent in handling people. Renata Castro is fluent in all the above.

FOREWORD

Have you heard of the term accidental entrepreneur? Pleasure to meet you, I am Mariana Barbosa, and I am an accidental entrepreneur. In my search for meaning, and for a way to pay my bills, I began an incredible journey which resulted in an international company with offices in three countries: Portugal, Brazil, and the United States. Lytron Strategic was born out of luck and chance. https://lytronstrategic.com. now focuses its work in utilizing technology to optimize sales processes and help business owners get more leads, and make more money.

When your job is to get business owners more leads, and, as a result, more money, you develop an innate sense of what is wrong with businesses. This is a key factor in the success of a business, as many people only focus on getting more calls, more likes, or more people through the door, instead of focusing on operating their business more efficiently or profitably, improving their marketing efforts, or finding the right sources of financing.

This is unquestionably important, but the real key to faster entrepreneurial success, as I have observed time and time again, is to start your business off right, using tools like a business plan and the advice of professionals who contribute to the brain trust that will avoid aches and pains on the (at times) tortuous road on which an entrepreneur travels.

Planning is a requirement for a business **anywhere** in the world, but when the success of your business is directly attached to the well-being of your family because of a visa application, the stakes are much higher, and failure is certainly not an option. As an accidental entrepreneur, I lost valuable time and money as I asked the wrong questions and, as a result, ended up with the wrong answers. This was my case, however, I have good news for you — <u>**it doesn't have to be the same for you**</u>.

See, when I became an accidental entrepreneur, my brilliant friend and Immigration Attorney Renata Castro (yes, I am fangirling her) had not written this incredibly useful book with the equally brilliant James Chittenden. The two of them have summarized thousands of conversations about starting, marketing, financing, and operating a business to create a roadmap which leads you to a path of freedom and success in your new business endeavor.

Use these 99 questions to begin your journey. As you work on the questions and obtain the right answers, being an entrepreneur in the world's most competitive market and living your American Dream can become a reality.

Mariana Barbosa
Founder, Lytron
https://lytronstrategic.com

PRAISE FOR 99 QUESTIONS TO ASK BEFORE STARTING A BUSINESS IN THE US

"Being an entrepreneur in the world's most exciting market is one step closer to being a reality for those who read this book."

- **Elizabeth Alderete**, President of the Brazilian Business Group

"'If you can't find a way, make one.' I've always been fond of this can-do, proactive approach to life and business. These 99 Questions are certainly a catalyst to do the research and organize your plans - to find your way. And, when combined with the entrepreneurial drive, capitalist business spirit, and execution of your business plan - you'll make one."

- **Ryan Jon Orner** - Experienced Investment Banker, Private Capital Investor, and Strategic Advisor to Middle Market Companies; Former Adjunct Professor of Finance at FSU

"Seldom do start-ups correctly forecast the finances, day-to-day operation costs, or funds needed to scale successfully. The questions presented here provide valuable insight on being better prepared when launching a business."

- **Edayat Shahrani**, Finance Professor, University of Tampa

"Aspiring to engage in an entrepreneurial endeavor is much more palatable for those who ask the right questions – such as the ones proposed in this useful book."

- **Joe Gomes**, CPA Partner at RVG & Co.

"In my years advising foreign nationals looking to move to the U.S. as a Certified Public Accountant, it is without question that I say – asking these questions from the beginning of the process will avoid unnecessary headaches. Renata and James hit a homerun for investors looking to live their American Dream."

- **Fernando Mello**, Business Broker, Transworld

"Business ownership is the first step up and out of generational poverty. As the granddaughter of immigrants who rolled cigars in Ybor City (Florida), I watched them work to make others wealthy. Working ten hour days is the easy part for many of us. It's the business end that can be complicated. This book clearly defines the steps to a lifetime of financial freedom! Good luck!"

- **Senator Janet Cruz**, Florida State Senate

INTRODUCTION

Renata

"This defines entrepreneur and entrepreneurship – the entrepreneur always searches for change, responds to it, and exploits it as an opportunity," wrote **Peter Drucker**, in his book *Innovation and Entrepreneurship: Practice and Principles*.

Being an immigrant, thus, should be synonymous with being an entrepreneur, as an individual leaves his home, his country, his language, his family, and all the other cultural ties which are meaningful to him or her – all for the thrill of pursuing the unknown. Some move to the U.S. for personal reasons, but most want the excitement and challenge of being an entrepreneur in the world's most dynamic and resilient economy.

This isn't just a theory; more than two-fifths of all Fortune 500 companies were founded by immigrants and their children.

Because an entrepreneur is open to change, and responds to it, James and I decided that entrepreneurs – particularly foreign entrepreneurs – needed a roadmap of where to begin their American Dream. And then and there this book was born.

Unequivocally, the entrepreneurial road begins with questions. Can I live a different life? Can I make a difference by selling my services or products? Do I have what it takes to be an entrepreneur? These may sound like philosophical questions, but as a business takes shape, the depth and importance of these questions become central to the success of the business.

It was amazing for me to hear from James, time and time again, how entrepreneurs were failing not because they did not have the skill, or the grit, but because they were not asking the right questions. After consulting with over three thousand (3,000!) business owners, it's safe to conclude that James knows a thing or two (or thousands) about what makes a business successful. Asking the right questions will lead you down a road where you find the right answers, and we both concluded that many aspiring entrepreneurs were going on a trip without a roadmap, GPS, or even a flashlight. All because they did not know which questions to ask.

We initially agreed on 99 questions, however, as James and I discussed the essential issues which infallibly plagued foreign entrepreneurs in their pursuit of business success in America, we had an abundance of vitally important questions. It was really a duel of titans to see which one of us came up with the most essential question.

This book brings me one step closer to my professional goal as an attorney: to be a part of the dream of as many foreigners who, like myself, took a leap of faith and came to the land of the free and the home of the brave in their pursuit of happiness, challenge, and growth.

As an entrepreneur myself, it is my hope that this book will help you avoid many of the mistakes I made when launching my practice, which despite being wildly successful, baptized me with the fire of entrepreneurial naïveté and inexperience. Castro Legal Group has grown double digits each year since its establishment, and this is testimony to my commitment to experimenting, learning, and achieving, both in law and in business.

As a human being, I co-wrote this book because I just want you, our reader, to experience the magical, indescribable experience of seeing your dream come true. My business gives me that opportunity every single day when I open the door to my office, and when I see that it is possible to make a living by fulfilling one's purpose.

James

Our intent is that the modest price you paid for this book will be returned to you in large multiples. We will do that by saving you a great deal of time, money, and pain from mistakes that you will avoid with our help. Even better, you will discover ways to make your new business operationally easier and more profitable.

This book will guide you through the planning of a new business and life. In the end, however, you may decide *not* to start a particular business. You may decide to take another path. Or you may find a renewed confidence in your plan. Either way is fine.

This book will help you clarify for yourself why you are entering a business, and why others should enter it with you. It will also help you clarify *who* should join you.

Nobody gets involved in your plans or projects without a reward. People may be rewarded financially or otherwise, and such rewards are most likely to be exchanged among those who are like-minded as you. This book will help you to identify those people and create a business that makes your customers happy and provides a good living for you, your family, your employees, and your business partners.

The 80/20 rule applies to entrepreneurs like much else in life. Eighty percent of businesses that start today in the United States will not exist five years from today. I was a small business banker and consultant who sat with thousands of business owners and taught thousands more, and it became easy to see why so many businesses fail. Many would-be entrepreneurs lack business skills that are easily learned or delegated to someone. To be one of the twenty percent who will be in business and doing well, start asking the right questions in order to arrive at the right place.

A business consultant can be as popular as the Grinch who stole Christmas. We must prod you to do tasks that are decidedly dreary. Break-even analysis, bookkeeping, setting sales goals, pricing, and other essential tasks are not what you had in mind when you started your business. In-depth expertise in such skills is not required, but working knowledge is. The best managers always have the right information right at their fingertips. The best way to have that sort of knowledge is to know the business like the back of your hand. And the best way to know the business like the back of your hand is creating and raising it. It's your baby.

One more thing. If you come across a term that you are unfamiliar with, stop and look it up. For example, you will see some immigration pathways in this book such as EB-2, EB-5, etc. Chapter 3 explains what those are.

Why 99 Questions?

The goal of this book is simple: guiding you to ask the right questions. You will find that when you ask questions and develop answers, more questions will arise. These 99 questions are more than sufficient to get you started.

As a business owner, your questions and challenges are sorted into four main areas:

- **Starting your business**, because it takes guts and courage to go on a path of entrepreneurship and independence. It takes seeing the forest for the trees. It takes imagining a path, and a life, which isn't there at the beginning.
- **Marketing your business** will be an ongoing challenge to solve repeatedly, because all businesses must get people through the door on a daily basis who are willing to sign on the dotted line. *Marketing brings in the customers.*
- **Operating your business** and learning the rhythmic heartbeat of your business when it is functioning properly,

helps you find new efficiencies and build momentum that can lead to further successes. *Operations keeps the customers.*
- **Financing your business** makes the magic happen, as much needed cash is required to move your business vision from abstract to concrete. *Finance keeps score and keeps you paid.*

Of course, these topics can, and frequently do, overlap. A financial problem may actually be a marketing problem in disguise. You don't have enough money to pay bills because you aren't selling enough. Operational decisions show up in the finances of the business, as another example.

And then there are the life questions about immigrating to America, starting a business, or both. Ask the right questions, get the right answers, repeat as necessary. Questions will lead you to answers you may not like, but that's OK. In fact, the very process of business planning is asking and answering questions.

The bad answers? Consider them a memo pad. They alert you to pitfalls. They expose weaknesses or vulnerabilities in your plan that need to be strengthened or avoided altogether. Solving those problems increases your profits and decreases your losses and expenses.

You will find that this book provides you with a plan for business and for life – all on your terms. You will uncover knowledge that was always yours anyway. We're just here to help you discover it.

How to Best Use This Book

Many are the times individuals seek the help of a professional — business consultant, attorney, accountant – only to find that the time they have allotted to speak to the professional during a consultation was not sufficient to address all the key aspects of the new endeavor, especially the legal implications.

So instead of using that time effectively, your valuable money and time were wasted discussing things which were not directly relevant to the task at hand: deciding whether to start a business in the U.S.

This book should be a guide. A reference. A place where you make notes. Lots of notes! Keep in mind that everyone learns differently, so feel free to use this book in the way which best suits you.

However, we'd encourage you to at least **try** this method:

- Read the book in its entirety and circle all the questions which are relevant to your particular situation.

- Go back to the questions that you marked and write down your thoughts, questions, or comments.
- Go to https://www.oneclickadvisor.com and select a professional in the Referral Network (or any other professional you trust) and, during your scheduled time, discuss the notes on your questions relevant to the professional's area of expertise.

  ○ Make sure to add the professional's suggestions to your notes relating to the specific questions.

- Read the book again, this time with your notes, and decide on a plan of action.

Even though this book contains a summary of years of experience between both authors, the learning does not end here. Go to oneclickadvisor.com and sign up to receive the free newsletter. Subscribe to One Click Advisor on YouTube. Send us questions on Facebook or Instagram. We want to know more about your journey as you decide to move one step closer to your American Dream.

Glossary of Investment-Related Visas

If you do not live in the U.S., your decision to purchase this book was motivated, at least in part, by the fact that you and your family wish to reside in the United States. In order to do that, aside from choosing a house, a car, and boarding a plane, there's a very important thing you **must** obtain — a visa which allows you to engage in the type of activity in which you wish to engage. What does that legalese mean to you, dear reader? It means that you must obtain a visa which allows you to work in the U.S. if you wish to work and allows you to come and go if that is what you want.

Different types of visas offer different legal rights and opportunities and changing your mind later may create unnecessary obstacles for you and your family. Planning for a visa, the right way, from the get-go, makes a great difference in whether or not you and your family will live your American Dream, or become entangled in a costly nightmare.

Below you will find a list of the common types of visas and descriptions of their eligibility requirements. Renata is a practicing immigration attorney, and these definitions are based on U.S. law, the Immigration and Nationality Act ("INA"), and other legally controlling acts as of the time of publishing. Other answers can be drawn from the *Code of Federal Regulations (C.F.R.)*, frequently cited below. Even though these summaries are intended to be informative, they are no substitute for personalized, professional legal advice. You can find a directory of licensed attorneys at www.oneclickadvisor.com under the Referral Network link.

Non-immigrant visas

- E-1

Citizens of a treaty country can be admitted to the U.S. under an E-1 classification for the sole purpose of engaging in international trade on their behalf, although certain employees of such a person, or of a qualifying organization, may also be eligible for the immigration benefit.

To obtain the benefit, the applicant (also known as a *treaty trader*), must be a national of the qualifying country; carry on substantial trade; and carry on principal trade between the U.S. and the qualifying country. The INA describes trade as *the existing international exchange of items of trade for consideration between the USA and the treaty country.* The trade may be in goods, services, international banking, insurance, tourism, technology and its transfer, or certain news-gathering activities, to cite a few. 8 C.F.R. 214.2(e)(9) provides additional examples and discussion. It is important to note that principal trade between the USA and the treaty country exists when over 50% of the volume of international trade of the treaty trader is between the

U.S. and the treaty country of the treaty trader's nationality. 8 C.F.R. 214.2(e)(11).

Traders, employees, and dependents are allowed a maximum initial stay of two years; extensions may be granted in two-year increments. It is important to note that the E-1 treaty trader **must** maintain the intent to depart the USA when their status of visa expires or is terminated.

- E-2

Obtaining an E-2 is possible for citizens of a treaty country who invest a substantial amount of capital in an American business which can be an existing or a new enterprise. The investor must show that he or she is a passport-holder (and therefore a citizen) of one of the treaty countries; that he or she has invested or is actively in the process of investing a substantial amount of capital in a bona fide enterprise in the U.S.; and that he or she is seeking to enter the U.S. solely to develop and direct the investment enterprise. The foreign investor must show at least 50% of the enterprise or possession of operational control through a managerial position or other corporate device.

Although the law does not define a minimum investment amount, it does say that a "substantial amount of capital" is required. Substantial amount of capital is defined as a sum which is substantial in relationship to the total cost of either purchasing an established enterprise or establishing a new business, *or* sufficient to ensure the treaty investor's financial commitment to the successful operation of the enterprise, *or* an amount of capital of a magnitude to support the likelihood that the treaty investor will successfully develop and direct the enterprise. The less money required to start or acquire the business overall, the less money will be needed to meet the "substantial amount" threshold.

Finally, the business must be a bona fide enterprise, which is one which is real, active, and engaged in the course of operating a commercial or entrepreneurial undertaking which produces services or goods for profit.

The visa is valid for 5 years, however, the E-2 applicant and his or her dependents must renew their authorized stay every two years. Notice of any fundamental change in the operation of the E-2 enterprise must be provided to the United States Citizenship and Immigration Services ("USCIS"), and could affect visa eligibility.

- L-1A

Those seeking L-1A visa classification must show that a U.S. employer is looking to transfer an executive or manager from one of its foreign offices to its existing U.S. location. It is also possible to send a manager or executive to develop the operation of a new U.S.-based office, but in that case it will be crucial to keep a timeline of development in order to maintain eligibility for the renewal of the visa.

Only the employer can request the immigration benefit, and the employee must show that he or she has held a qualifying relationship with the foreign company *and* that he or she either is currently or will be doing business for the employer in the U.S. which still owns and operates one or more offices abroad.

The executive or manager must prove that he or she has been working for the foreign company for at least one continuous year in the three-year period immediately preceding the admission to the U.S., and that he or she will be an executive or manager of the US operations for the enterprise.

The foreign company must be a parent company, branch, subsidiary, or affiliate of the U.S. company.

An executive is someone who has broad authority to make decisions in the enterprise. A manager is someone who supervises and controls the work of professional employees. A manager is also someone who manages the organization, or a department, subdivision, function, or component of the organization. Lack of supervision of the manager or executive is a key factor in determining whether or not the employee is a manager or executive as described in section 101(a)44 of the Immigration and Nationality Act, as amended. For complete definitions, see 8 CFR 214.2(l)(1)(ii).

Unlike all of the other non-immigrant visas, this visa classification creates a direct pathway to a green card under EB-1C classification. Note that receiving an L-1A visa does not guarantee the ultimate receipt of a green card; it merely creates a likely path of eligibility.

- B1

A temporary business visitor can engage in business activities of a commercial or professional nature, such as consulting with business associates; traveling to the U.S. for a scientific, educational, professional, or business convention or conference with specific dates; settling an estate; negotiations of a contract; or short-term training; to name a few.

There is no minimum period of time for which a B-1 visa can be issued, but the longest a B-1 visa is issued is 10 years. A B-1 visa holder usually receives a 6-month period of authorized stay every time he or she seeks entry to the U.S.

This is the most limited of all investment-related visas, and the consular agent has broad discretion in approving or denying a B-1 visa based on the purpose of the trip, the applicant's overall financial adequacy to cover the expenses of the trip, and all ties to the applicant's country of residence. In sum, consular agents want reassurances that the B-1 visa holder will return to their home country after a trip to the U.S.

- International Entrepreneur Parole Rule

Unlike the other programs which have a set period for issuance, the International Entrepreneur Parole Rule allows the Department of Homeland Security to invoke its parole authority to grant a period of authorized stay, on a case-by-case basis, to foreign entrepreneurs who can show that they would bring a significant public benefit by opening or operating a business in the U.S., and they deserve an approval in order to open or operate the proposed enterprise.

The foreign investor can only work on their designated business, but spouses can obtain authorization to work for any employer once in the U.S. Children of the foreign investor are not eligible to obtain employment authorization.

A peculiar feature of the International Entrepreneur Parole Rule is that up to three entrepreneurs can petition for the immigration privilege per enterprise.

The applicant must show that he or she has substantial ownership in a start-up entity that was created in the past five years, and that the enterprise has substantial potential for rapid growth and job creation.

The applicant must also show that he or she will have an active and central role in the start-up, and that they are well-positioned to assist in the growth and success of the enterprise. Investment money alone is not enough.

In addition, the applicant must show that there will be a benefit to the U.S. resulting from their role as an entrepreneur, such as receiving a significant amount in investment capital, receipt of grants or awards for economic development, research and development or job creation from federal, state, or local government entities, or that the enterprise partially meets either one or both previous requirements, and that the applicant can provide reliable and compelling evidence of the enterprise's potential for rapid growth and job creation.

- O-1A

Those seeking O-1A visa classification must show that he or she is an alien of extraordinary ability in the sciences, arts, education, business, or athletics. A showing of sustained national or international acclaim is required, and the foreign entrepreneur must show that he or she will enter the U.S. to continue engaging in their area of expertise. Because this application is one not attached to an investment, but to the actual qualifications of the foreign alien, the individual must show that he or she will have a contract with the petitioning enterprise; evidence of their extraordinary achievements such as awards, publications, patents; and any other type of comparable evidence that shows, in the totality of the evidence, that a favorable decision is warranted; and that the foreign entrepreneur has risen to the very top of their field nationally or internationally.

Immigrant visas (Green Card)

- EB-1A

Known as the "Einstein Visa", the EB-1A classification is reserved for those who have reached the highest achievements in their profession, be it in the arts, sciences, education, business, or athletics. By showing that the applicant has enjoyed national or international acclaim, the applicant can obtain a green card, along with his or her spouse and children under 21 years old, which will allow the family to live, invest, study, and engage in any commercial activity in the U.S.

The applicant must prove that he or she meets 3 out of 10 legal criteria as set forth below, or that he or she has received a major one-time achievement, such as an Oscar, a Pulitzer Prize, or an Olympic Medal.

Although there is no legal requirement that the applicant should make an investment, the petition must show that he or she will continue to work in the area of their expertise, although an offer of employment or labor certification is not required.

If the applicant does not fulfill the one-time achievement prong, he or she must show, through evidence, at least 3 of the following criteria:

1. Receipt of lesser nationally or internationally recognized prizes or awards for excellence;
2. Membership in associations in the field which demand outstanding achievement of their members;
3. Published material about the applicant in professional or major trade publications or other major media;
4. The applicant has been asked to judge the work of others in the same field, either individually or on a panel;
5. The applicant's original scientific, scholarly, artistic, athletic, or business-related contributions of major significance to the field;
6. The applicant's authorship of scholarly articles in professional or major trade publications or other major media;
7. The applicant's work has been displayed at artistic exhibitions or showcases;
8. The applicant's performance of a leading or critical role in distinguished organizations;
9. The applicant commands a high salary or other significantly high remuneration in relation to others in the field;
10. The applicant's commercial successes in the performing arts.

- **EB-1C**

Certain multinational managers or executives, particularly those who have entered the U.S. under an L-1A classification, may have their employers petition for their green card without the requirement of a labor certification, as long as the beneficiary of the application has been employed for the employer outside the U.S. for at least one of the three years preceding either the green card application or the non-immigrant visa application. The U.S. employer must have been doing business for at least one year in the U.S., and have a qualifying relationship to the affiliated entity abroad where the beneficiary held or holds a managerial or executive position.

Although no investment is required by the beneficiary, the petitioning company (which could be owned by the beneficiary), must show that its operations are viable in the U.S.

Much like the EB-1A petition, spouses and minor single children receive the immigration benefit along with the principal beneficiary.

- EB-2/ NIW

An individual of extraordinary ability may seek a waiver of a labor certification if he can show that his skills and proposed endeavor are in the national interest of the U.S.

A National Interest Waiver ("NIW") does not require an investment nor the opening of a business, however, it is common to have the proposed endeavor be attached to a new enterprise which will result, among other things, in job creation for the American economy. The EB-2/NIW visa is not a visa for jobs program. Instead, the U.S. government waives the requirement for a labor certification attached to a job offer by a U.S.-based employer if the applicant can show that his proposed endeavor is one that has both substantial merit and national importance, that he is well positioned to advance the proposed endeavor, and that it would be beneficial to the U.S. to waive the requirements of a job offer. The applicant must comply with three of the seven criteria set forth below:

1. Evidence of a degree, diploma, certificate, or similar award related to the area of exceptional ability;
2. Letters documenting at least 10 years of full-time experience in the area of exceptional ability;
3. A license to practice the profession or certification for the profession or occupation in question;
4. Evidence that the applicant has commanded a salary or other remuneration for services that demonstrates the applicant's exceptional ability;
5. Membership in a professional association;
6. Recognition for achievements and significant contributions to the applicant's industry or field by peers, government entities, professional or business organizations;
7. Other comparable evidence of eligibility is also acceptable.

- EB-5

Investors who make the necessary investment in a Direct or Regional Center Investment, as defined below, which results in the creation or preservation of 10 or more full-time jobs, may receive a green card through the EB-5 program, also known as the "visa for jobs" program.

A Direct Investment is one where the foreign investor is directly involved in the management and operation of the job-creating enterprise; a Regional Center Investment is one where the foreign investor isn't involved in the running of the enterprise. In addition, under a Regional Center Investment, the foreign investor must show job creation through an economic output, as this investment model allows for accounting of direct, indirect, and induced jobs.

The minimum investment amount has changed rather frequently.

THE 99 Questions

Here they are. Not all of them will be applicable to you. When you find one that is, use the page as a journal to write your answers.

1. **When you were 4 years old, what did you want to be when you grew up and why?**

James Chittenden ("JC"): Children of that age have ideas of what adults do that seem heroic or interesting. They lionize certain professions and the people who work in them. For example, a four-year-old boy may think he wants to be a firefighter. It isn't the job that attracts the boy. It is what the job *represents* that attracts the boy. So whatever adult job you thought you wanted as a four-year old, ask yourself why that excited you. That matters today because it is a significant personal clue for working and living.

2. How would your life change if you were running a business in the U.S.?

JC: Consider the positive changes and the negatives as well. A new market like the U.S., as exciting as it sounds, also brings its challenges such as language and cultural barriers, as well as new trade dynamics which may prove challenging. After working with thousands of foreigners who are eager to start businesses in the U.S., my suggestion is that you do a brain dump of all the ways your life will change — for better or worse. Use this as a guideline to help you and all the people who will be impacted by this endeavor (family and business partners, for example) discuss if the good outweighs the bad.

3. What does being an entrepreneur mean to you?

JC: Is it freedom? Financial security? Recognition? Deprivation? Risk? Write down the very first things that come to mind. They represent what you hope to gain *and* what you hope to avoid.

4. What do you want your life to look like in one year?

JC: Finances? Health? Location? Job or business? Write your answers not for today's day and month, but for next year. Moving abroad is *not* a project to take lightly, let alone one where a change of country and entrepreneurial environment are at stake. Be realistic, but hopeful.

5. Do you have a vision in mind?

JC: You may have a business in mind, and an idea of how it should run. You may or may not have a business plan. If not, start developing one. It does not have to be elaborate, nor an academic exercise. After all, Southwest Airlines started as an idea written on the back of a cocktail napkin. Sort your questions into one of the following areas: starting your business, marketing your business, operating your business, or financing your business.

6. Do you have a business in mind?

JC: Write down your chosen industry.

Renata Castro ("RC"): This is always a tough one. Foreign entrepreneurs come speak to my team and me at Castro Legal Group to discuss visas, but they rarely have an idea of what specific kind of business they want to run. Immigration lawyers rarely have the business acumen to discuss the best endeavor to engage in. However, a visa is only available for those seeking an investment-based visa, *if* the proposed business is a success. Discussing the viability of the business with a business consultant before speaking to an immigration attorney expedites the process of successfully completing the application with the USCIS, or the designated consulate or embassy.

7. Do you have a timeline?

JC: This page is an excellent place to start setting a timetable for various milestones. Applying for a visa is a milestone. Acquiring sufficient funds to start a business is a milestone. Incorporating is a milestone. What are the most important actions you must take, and when do you hope to accomplish them?

RC: Keep in mind that the U.S. government moves at the speed of a turtle crawling uphill. Planning for delays can help avoid the personal heartbreak and financial losses that can come with unrealistic timelines for those looking to start a business in the U.S. and receive an immigration benefit.

8. What kind of business structure should you have?

JC: You can choose between a sole proprietorship, partnership, limited liability company (LLC), or corporation. To learn the advantages and disadvantages of each, see the "Start Your Business" page on the One Click Advisor website at www.oneclickadvisor.com. For more specialized help, visit the One Click Advisor Referral Network, where you can find legal, accounting, and tax guidance for your unique situation.

9. Will you need a physical facility?

JC: How much space will you need for operations, employee offices, sales floor areas, warehouses and other storage, or other business functions? Many new business owners are relieved to learn that they do not need to enter into multi-year leases for office, warehouse, food services, or other facilities. Co-working, subletting, shared commercial kitchens, and other short-term facilities offer affordable month-to-month options.

RC: Most visa petitions will require obtaining a physical facility, even if it's just a shared office space, to operate your business. Home-based visas can be an option, as long as you obtain an occupational license and there is enough space to house the needs of the enterprise. **HOWEVER**, this is, in my opinion, a bad move. More often than not, USCIS frowns upon the usage of a home office.

10. How do you plan to fund this business?

JC: There are many ways to fund your business other than a bank loan. You can fund a business with credit cards, personal funds, investor capital, or lesser-known methods such as selling receivables. There are also the "Three F's", which are "Friends, Family, and Fools." Record your ideas here.

11. If you are married, how does your spouse feel about moving to the U.S.?

RC: Everyone's relationship is different, but in all these years practicing immigration law, I have heard more times than I would like to count the tale of the husband who will leave the family abroad while traveling back and forth. *This rarely works.* Be prepared to have these discussions in the beginning of your process, as immigration procedures are rather bureaucratic and morose, and last minute or fast issuance of visas are rarely possible. So if your spouse initially decides to stay abroad, but later changes his or her mind, you should expect potentially substantial delays in your visas being issued.

12. If you are married, how does your spouse feel about you becoming an entrepreneur?

JC: Be honest about your spouse's position regarding your proposed venture. This is an opportunity to account for your spouse's concerns and involve your spouse in your plan.

13. Will your spouse be involved in the running of the business?

JC: Consider the role of your spouse in the business. It is necessary to have uncomfortable conversations about setting agreements in the event of divorce or dissolution of the business. As painful as it might be, it's far less painful to talk about these issues now than trying to litigate them afterwards.

RC: It is always tempting to add your spouse to your budding enterprise, in an effort to keep revenue growth within your household, particularly for businesses with a low initial capital investment. However, the US government wants to see foreign entrepreneurs create jobs for people already in the U.S. and looking for employment. Your spouse is likely NOT one of them. Moreover, in some cases, job creation is a cornerstone of obtaining your immigration benefit, such as in an EB-5 petition. In this case, 10 jobs must be created per investor, and the jobs created for family members are NOT counted towards the required number.

14. If you are not already an entrepreneur abroad, what's stopping you?

JC: If there is another country you are well familiar with, there may be reasons why your proposed business isn't as feasible there. What are those reasons?

RC: The allure to becoming an entrepreneur in the U.S. is rather enticing, however, entrepreneurship is a challenge no matter the geographic location. I am sorry to be the bearer of bad news, but there are no dollar trees behind our homes, or offices, or places of business. Are you prepared to put in the necessary hustle to make your business work?

15. Where would your business be located?

JC: This should be a city and state, or multiple locations, or online. *Where* you are matters as much as *what* you are.

16. Where do you want to live in the U.S.?

JC: City and state. Maybe even a specific neighborhood or area of town. Make it specific. Take airports into consideration, for example, if you will continue to go abroad frequently for work or to visit family and friends.

17. How much will it take for you to live during the first twelve months?

JC: Add up all your personal bills, plus sufficient "miscellaneous" expenses to arrive at an amount you need to live on each month, in U.S. dollars. Multiply by 12.

18. How will you pay for your personal expenses in the first twelve months of operations?

JC: Have a job or other personal financing in place.

RC: Many investment-based visas, such as the E-2, do not allow for the investor to work in any other job aside from the enterprise. Therefore, having a Plan B for revenue may avoid legal violations of your immigration status.

19. What does financial success in this business look like?

JC: Set a revenue goal that pays the bills of the business, allows you to make a suitable living for yourself and your family, and provides a healthy profit. How much is that each month? Calculate a specific dollar amount.

20. Will you need a visa to operate this business?

RC: Tourist/Business Visas B1/B2 can allow an individual to own a business in the U.S., contrary to popular belief. However, the scope of what is allowed is narrow.

A B1 visa holder can only consult with business associates; travel for a scientific, educational, professional or business convention, or a conference on specific dates; settle an estate; negotiate a contract; or participate in short term training. However, a B1 visa holder cannot engage in the active management and running of a U.S.-based business. Therefore, if you will need to personally put in the initial work to run the business, a different type of visa, one which allows for such activity, will be required.

21. What will it take for you to qualify for a visa?

RC: The mere willingness to open a business is not enough to obtain a visa. Before opening your business, or making any investment, you **must** consult with an immigration attorney. Path of funds, compliance, and job creation requirements are all important elements of a successful investment-based visa application.

22. How long will it take to get the visa?

RC: Some visa categories allow for premium processing, which is a fee in exchange for a faster processing of your case. This does *not* mean the case will be approved because you paid the additional fee, nor that it will be approved in the time period you need to be in the U.S. for whatever reason — even for the business. Therefore, discussing realistic timelines with your immigration attorney is a key step in properly executing your plan to become an entrepreneur in the U.S.

Renata Castro, Esq., James Chittenden

23. How much will it cost for you to qualify for a visa?

RC: Beyond just the direct investment in the business, investment-based visas can have costs such as immigration attorneys, business attorneys, CPAs or accountants, business consultants, translation services, and corporate filing fees – just to name a few. These costs may be considered a part of the investment, however, the amount invested must still be sufficient to make the business viable.

Immigration law is a matter of federal jurisdiction, therefore, you have the ability to hire a lawyer to represent you anywhere in the United States. This gives you the ability to choose the best representation irrespective of the physical location of the lawyer. It is important to plan accordingly, to avoid unnecessary surprises and budget shortcomings in such an essential expenditure to the business. The complexity of your personal, family, and business' specific situations will have a direct impact on the legal fees.

24. What happens to your visa if your business goes bust?

RC: When the business goes bust matters just as much as if the business no longer exists. Each investment visa will impose a different criteria. If you are petitioning for an investment-based green card, such as an EB-2/NIW, an EB-5, or an EB-1C, if the business closes **after** the green card is approved and issued, the longevity of the business no longer impacts the eligibility for an immigration benefit.

On the other hand, if applying for a non-immigrant visa such as an E-2, your lawful status is directly attached to the existence of the business. Therefore, no business, no visa – once the business closes, your eligibility for the visa ends.

25. Can you obtain all business licenses required with the visa category for which you qualify?

RC: Certain licenses, such as liquor and healthcare licenses, may be restricted to individuals with a certain immigration status, or a social security number, or both. To avoid an impasse, the establishment of the type of business you will own is just as important as the visa you seek with the assistance of your immigration attorney. It is advisable that you discuss with a business consultant all the aspects related to the opening and operating of your business, as the scope of services of an immigration attorney is usually limited to advising and petitioning for immigration benefits.

26. Who in your family will qualify for a visa as your dependent?

RC: Only direct relatives — husband, wife, and children who are single and under 21 – qualify as dependents for immigration purposes. If you have elderly parents, or other individuals under your care such as nephews, nieces, or cousins, it is important to acknowledge that they will have to seek their own independent basis for a visa, and planning may be required with an immigration attorney to discuss viable and legal options for your family member.

27. Who is your target audience? Is your end customer a consumer, a business, or a government?

JC: These categories are commonly referred to as business to business (B2B), business to consumer (B2C), or business to government (B2G). Your primary marketing efforts will fall under one of these categories.

28. Are there government subsidies available for your industry?

JC: This is rare, but subsidies can be available for farms and also for vital medical, scientific, or technological businesses.

29. Have you operated in this market abroad? What were your biggest challenges?

JC: Results in one country are often not a reliable indicator of similar results in another. Cultures vary, and therefore so do preferences for various goods and services. Write down some insights from doing business in your home country or in another country that could help you succeed in the U.S.

30. Do you speak enough English to operate this business?

RC: Visas are not contingent upon fluency in English, however, many entrepreneurs find that significant challenges arise from not being fluent in English and therefore relying on the expertise of employees or constantly paying for translation services. This can be a serious and expensive challenge, and one which you, the business owner, must take into consideration when deciding the type of business you want to engage in.

31. How much time will you have to physically be in the U.S. to operate this business?

RC: Most businesses, especially food service or retail, require a substantial owner presence, especially during the early stages.

32. Will you have employees? If so, when do you need to start hiring? And how many?

JC: It isn't always easy to time the hiring of employees. Don't hire too soon and don't hire too late. Tie the hiring of employees to sales projections, hiring as your revenue progresses.

RC: Hiring of employees may have a direct impact on your eligibility to obtain a visa. Discuss with your immigration attorney specific requirements before finalizing your investment.

33. Does your visa category require the hiring of employees?

RC: If you learn nothing from this book, learn this: the U.S. government did not design immigration laws in line with best business practices. Why do I say that? You may be required to hire employees even before you have generated dollar one in revenue in order to pursue an immigration benefit. This is the case for L-1s, E-2s, and EB-1Cs. EB-2/NIW petitions may use the job creation to partially satisfy the requirement of substantial merit, or national importance, or both. EB-5 applications have up to 2 years from the date of approval to show job creation for each investor of up to 10 full time jobs.

34. Which business licenses will you need to operate this business?

JC: Some businesses require licenses and others do not. Food services, healthcare, financial, heavy machinery, and businesses with an environmental impact are generally regulated. So, if the business poses a risk to the environment, community well-being, public or personal health, chances are far greater that licensing will be required. For example, barbers and cosmetologists use sharp objects and chemicals on customers, so your state will likely require licensing. A marketing company, on the other hand, will not.

35. If you're planning to use a home office, does your local government allow you to do so?

JC: If there is minimal traffic or impact on a neighborhood, a home office will not be a problem, generally speaking. However, if a business begins to generate traffic and impacts neighbors, it may be necessary to call your city's zoning office for instructions. When you have these conversations, record the name of the official or employee that answers your questions, as well as the date and time the conversation happened. In fact, this page is an excellent place to do that. This offers you some protection in the event that you get cited for an inadvertent zoning violation.

36. If using a home office, does immigration allow for such operation?

RC: Foreign entrepreneurs find it rather challenging to accommodate business best practices to the requirements imposed by government agencies. Truth is, many successful businesses have started in garages; however, the U.S. government is not willing to gamble on that. Home based businesses can be allowed in some cases, IF the local laws allow a business to operate from a home (this is resolved with the city) and you can prove that the physical space can accommodate the operation of the business. I **discourage** (don't do it!) using a home office for any business owner looking to obtain an immigration benefit. The headache is not worth the savings. The US government favors investors who have "skin in the game", and who are more sophisticated entrepreneurs. Operating out of an office implies that the foreign entrepreneur has a better infrastructure to run a successful business. It is important to realize that the speed of business is not the speed of government and following certain guidelines such as getting physical and separate office space denotes your commitment to the success of the enterprise.

Renata Castro, Esq., James Chittenden

37. What are you willing or not willing to compromise to own a business? What are your non-negotiables?

JC: Write down what your business will not do. Examples include but are not limited to: pollution or buying from countries with lax child labor laws. This is an opportunity to develop values-based guidelines for the business.

38. What are your family's non-negotiables?

JC: See question 37. Your business will be a family affair to some extent. However, values are personal and will vary among people in your family. What are some values that the family shares that could guide this business?

Renata Castro, Esq., James Chittenden

39. Why is the U.S. a desirable location for the operation of the business you have in mind?

JC: Is it culture? Laws? Location? Or is the U.S. where most of your customers are? Write down the advantages that the United States offers for your business above all others.

40. What are your thoughts about franchises?

JC: Are you willing to consider buying a business that operates under a system designed by others? This can be researched under One Click Advisor (Start Your Business).

Renata Castro, Esq., James Chittenden

41. What are the advantages of starting a business from scratch?

JC: You may have some ideas of the advantages of starting a brand new business. Write down as many as you can.

42. And what are the disadvantages?

JC: Clearly, you will be operating with some blind spots. Try to anticipate some and write them down. Be realistic. Do not avoid touching on challenging spots for fear of being negative. This is an opportunity for you to have an unvarnished bird's eye view of everything that could go wrong, so that you can make sure it goes right.

Renata Castro, Esq., James Chittenden

43. What are the advantages of owning a franchise?

JC: It depends on the franchise, but what appeals to you about buying a pre-existing system?

44. And what are the disadvantages of franchise ownership?

JC: Again, it depends on the franchise, but what worries you about buying a pre-existing system?

45. Will your U.S. business be linked to your business abroad, if you own any?

RC: L-1 visas require shared ownership between the two enterprises, therefore, if the goal is to petition for an L-1A for a Multinational Manager, an L-1B For a Specialized Knowledge employee, then shared ownership is a requirement. The same is not true for any other visa category.

46. Your life is perfect and you are operating a business you love – what does it look like?

JC: Write your ideal scene. Paint a word picture of your ideal work and personal life.

47. Will you have business partners? If so, who are they and what kind of role do they have in your business?

JC: What is your criteria for choosing partners, if any? Consider they type of people you are looking for. Do your strengths and weaknesses mesh well?

Relationships of all kinds work best if there is relative parity of intelligence, ethics, and mental health. The more equality of strength in those areas, the better.

Of course, human brains vary; someone with superior intelligence and aptitude for mechanics may lack computer programming aptitude, and vice versa. If two people have similar raw intelligence but complementary skills, they can form an effective partnership.

Ethics is personal; for example, health-conscious people and regular smokers are less likely to associate with one another.

Mental health; consider your own and that of a prospective partner as well.

48. If you choose to have business partners, what kind of business agreement will you have with them?

JC: A partnership agreement is like a premarital agreement. Agree on procedures in advance and put them in writing. There should be clear procedures in place to protect the business – and you – in the event of disputes or a partner's exit, divorce, death, or incapacitation.

49. Will your business partners need an immigration benefit?

RC: Some immigration options, like an E-2, require the visa applicant to be the controlling partner; therefore, having more than one investor apply in the same enterprise can be problematic. Visas like an EB-5, which require the creation of 10 or more jobs per investor, does not require a percentage of ownership in the enterprise, but does set forth minimum investment and job creation requirements per investor.

50. What kind of insurance will you need?

JC: Almost anything can be insured, but that does not mean that it should. After considering your acceptable and unacceptable risks, write down what is necessary to give you peace of mind.

For example, you can insure inventory against risks such as fire, theft, natural disasters, or other losses. You can obtain insurance for events that interrupt your business, such as the loss of a key manager or executive. You can obtain liability insurance and insurance for your premises as well.

Other insurance is mandatory under the laws of the state you will operate in. Expect required insurance coverage for workers' compensation and auto insurance if you operate vehicles. Additionally, if your property is in a designated flood zone, you may be required to purchase flood insurance.

One Click Advisor maintains a referral network that includes local insurance professionals. Otherwise, leading insurance platforms are available at https://www.oneclickadvisor.com/operations/.

Renata Castro, Esq., James Chittenden

51. Will your business require traveling?

JC: If so, travel will be a line item in the finances of your business. How much is necessary? Not all travel can be planned well in advance, but if travel is a regular feature of your business, plan accordingly.

52. How much traveling are you willing to do for your business?

JC: Is it necessary more or less in the beginning stages of your business? Traveling can get expensive. Also, travel and entertainment (commonly referred to as "T and E" by tax officials and tax professionals) are the most commonly scrutinized items in audits performed by the U.S. Internal Revenue Service ("IRS").

RC: Traveling abroad may not be possible until your immigration petition is approved, either in the U.S. for petitions under the jurisdiction of the USCIS, or a consulate or embassy abroad. It is important to plan in advance to avoid disruption to the course of business and losses. Please don't drive your immigration attorney crazy to try and expedite a process which cannot be expedited. Nothing replaces planning.

53. Do you know enough about the service or product you intend to sell to be able to set pricing?

JC: Are you familiar with the norms of your industry? Get familiar with them and write a range of prices that are charged by your competitors for the services or products you plan to sell, in the markets in which you plan to operate

54. What do you anticipate to be your top three challenges?

JC: Write down what you anticipate to be your main challenges as a business owner. They could be personal, professional, or both.

Renata Castro, Esq., James Chittenden

55. How will you reach your perfect client?

JC: First, you need to know who this ideal client is. Describe a "buyer persona." Male? Female? Age? Family or marital status? Household income? Area where this person lives? Once you know this, reaching them becomes a much simpler task.

56. Are you willing to engage the media? Why or why not?

JC: Consider this a test of your confidence in the strength and ethics of your business. If a reporter contacts you and is interested in covering your business, are you happy to accommodate the reporter? Or are you nervous about the idea? In my other book, ***The Public Triumph***, you can find extensive information on how to use media to promote your business. You can get the book for free. Only pay the cost of shipping and handling IF you use the QR code offer at the beginning of this book: *GET A COPY OF 'PUBLIC TRIUMPH' FOR FREE!*

57. Will you be selling products or services online?

JC: Write down your ideas for a digital marketing strategy. How will you attract attention for the business on the internet?

RC: There is a misconception that if your business is selling things online, that immigration laws and regulations do not apply because online is a lawless land. Even if you have an online business, U.S. laws apply and proper work authorization may be required. Discuss your business model with your immigration attorney.

58. If your product is perishable, will you be able to maintain sufficient inventory levels to fulfill orders?

JC: Write down products that you are selling that are perishable. Plan for a primary supplier, as well as at least two backup suppliers.

59. **If you are selling imported goods, do you need to adequate them to U.S. standards, such as compliance with the requirements of the U.S. Food and Drug Administration ("FDA")?**

JC: If you're selling food, find the U.S. Food and Drug Administration ("FDA") guidelines for importing food. Whatever you are selling, research U.S. government requirements and write them down here.

60. If selling a foreign product, will it violate U.S. patent or trademark laws?

JC: A U.S. copyright, trademark or patent search can be done online (a patent attorney is highly recommended, but not required). What are these?

Copyrights are the exclusive rights given to a creator to publish, print, perform, film or record literary, artistic, or musical material and to authorize others to do the same.

Trademarks are symbols or words legally registered or established to represent a product or company.

Patents are rights or licenses granted by the government that exclude others from making, using, or selling an invention.

61. If your product needs to be compliant with U.S. laws, how much time and money will it take to do that?

JC: Consult a foreign trade attorney if you do not have the answers readily available. Even better, contact the government agency, if any, responsible for regulating your chosen industry and ask them what is required. Unlike an attorney, answers from the government are free. Document who you talk to, the date, and what you were told. Write down what you know here.

62. Do you have a business plan? If not, do you need help writing one?

JC: Business plans are tantamount for the success of most, if not all investment-based visa applications. However, the business plan used for your visa application is rarely designed for the successful running of your business. Therefore, we recommend you have two business plans: one for immigration purposes and one for business purposes.

RC: The U.S. government and its immigration agencies are not in the business of running successful businesses. The landmark case *Matter of Ho* sets forth the minimum requirements for a business plan to be compliant for EB-5 cases, for example. However, this does *not* mean that this business plan will help you, as a foreign entrepreneur, to run your business. James and I agree that it may be in the best interest of your business to have two business plans – one for immigration purposes, and one for the day to day running of our business.

Renata Castro, Esq., James Chittenden

63. Will you maintain income sources from countries other than the U.S.?

JC & RC: We recommend an accountant that is familiar with laws in all countries from which you receive income. Accounting and tax professionals are available through many sources, including the One Click Advisor Professional Referral Service at

https://www.oneclickadvisor.com/referral-network-listing/

64. Will you become a tax resident of the U.S.?

JC: The U.S. tax code is very complex, and to avoid complications with what is essentially the world's most powerful debt collector, you want to discuss your options with a professional before your tax residency in the U.S. is established. Go to www.oneclickadvisor.com where you can find a list of professionals who can help you with a plan to minimize your tax exposure.

RC: The U.S. considers some individuals tax residents even if they are not legal residents of the U.S. The IRS considers an individual a tax resident if the person passes the Green Card test or the substantial presence test. Under the Green Card test, you are a tax resident if you were a lawful permanent resident of the U.S. at any time during the calendar year.

Tax residency under the substantial presence test is established if you spent 31 days during the current calendar year in the U.S. or its territory (including territorial waters), *and* your total presence in the U.S. adds up to 183 days during the 3 year period which includes the current year and the 2 years immediately before that, counting: all the days you were present in the current year, and ⅓ of the days you were present in the first year before the current year, and ⅙ of the days you were present in the second year before the current year.

Exemptions, although limited, are available. Tax planning is essential <u>before</u> beginning any immigration process to avoid unnecessary taxation to your worldwide income.

65. How will you handle bookkeeping?

JC: Write the name of a bookkeeper you are considering using, unless you have the skills and time to perform your own bookkeeping. A bookkeeper will reconcile your bank statements and generate your financial statements; specifically, your profit/loss (commonly known as an income statement), balance sheet, and cash flow statement.

The value of accurate bookkeeping is that your most up-to-date financial information is always at your fingertips. At a moment's notice, you can provide your complete financial picture to anyone who asks. This comes in handy when applying for loans or responding to an audit.

Bookkeeping products and services are available at https://www.oneclickadvisor.com/finance/, and bookkeepers and accountants are available through the One Click Advisor Referral Network.

66. Do you have an accounting system?

JC: You can either hire bookkeepers or do it yourself. In addition to accounting, an accounting platform can also perform functions such as payroll and invoicing. Be honest about your confidence in your skills to perform bookkeeping tasks. Your time as an entrepreneur is your most valuable asset, and using shortcuts like https://www.oneclickadvisor.com/finance/ to find bookkeeping products and services frees you up to handle more tasks. In the beginning, entrepreneurs tend to be a one-man show, and using your time effectively allows you to do more, and as a consequence, earn more.

Renata Castro, Esq., James Chittenden

67. Is your business seasonal?

JC: Many businesses are seasonal, with certain times of the year busier than others. You will need additional working capital and you may need to hire additional employees to get you through these seasons. Write down your anticipated needs during your most and least busy times.

For example, the busiest season of a vacation resort venue may be the months of June through August. By March, management should have plans in place for that busy season. That is the time to obtain a line of credit, to begin hiring and training seasonal or part-time help, ensure proper insurance, and obtain adequate supplies.

68. Do you have a disaster preparedness plan?

JC: At a minimum, this may consist of proper insurance and immediate access to two years of monthly financial statements for your business. Also, a list of assets and the value of these assets, complete with photographs will be very helpful in the event of an insurable loss. The reason you want to have such data readily available is because emergency loans may be available, and the financial statements are part of the emergency loan application. The sooner a complete application can be submitted, the sooner the application can be approved with funds disbursed to you.

Disaster relief loans from state governments are a regular occurrence in the U.S. However, approval and disbursement of funds takes time. Interest payments normally become due six months from the time of disbursement. If you have adequate insurance (for items such as business interruption, fire, flood, theft, loss of inventory, etc.), the policy may pay you well before payments become due on the emergency loan. In many cases, this enables you to pay off the emergency loan in full before payments become due, resulting in minimal or zero financial interruption to your business.

All of this is possible *only if* you keep financial statements up to date and maintain adequate insurance.

Renata Castro, Esq., James Chittenden

69. Do you plan to open a business bank account?

JC: Please note that the business must have a U.S. Employer Identification Number ("EIN") before a U.S. bank will allow your business to open an account. This number will be used to report taxes as well.

70. Are the names you have in mind available for registration in your state?

JC: Ensure that your business name is not in use, nor under U.S. trademark protection.

Renata Castro, Esq., James Chittenden

71. If the name is available, is the domain available for purchase?

JC: Simply check your domain registration site of choice and see if your preferred domain is available. The shorter and easier to remember, the better.

72. How will you obtain health insurance?

JC: There are many vendors for purchasing health insurance in the U.S. A group policy is preferable because discounts apply. Additionally, health insurance is a tax-deductible expense for your business if the business buys it on behalf of you and employees. One Click Advisor offers multiple opportunities to obtain adequate health insurance for U.S. citizens and non-citizens alike.

Renata Castro, Esq., James Chittenden

73. Can you obtain life insurance?

JC: Like health insurance, life insurance is a regular employee benefit due to tax laws and business norms in the U.S. Most people can obtain it fairly easily. One Click Advisor offers multiple opportunities to obtain adequate life insurance for U.S. citizens and non-citizens alike.

RC: Obtaining life insurance is possible even for individuals in the USA with a tourist visa like a B1/B2. Insurance companies set forth the requirements, and it is essential for peace of mind for you and your family. I encourage you to find a licensed insurance professional and discuss your needs.

74. Which payment terms will be available to your customers?

JC: If you are extending credit to your customers, write down the terms you are willing to offer them. They must not be longer than the terms your suppliers impose on you, or you will experience cash flow problems. For example, if your supplier must be paid in 30 days, but you allow your customers 45 day terms, you could be without funds for at least 15 days.

Renata Castro, Esq., James Chittenden

75. Will you need to speak a language other than English to operate your business?

JC: This is an operational concern more than a legal concern. Depending on your hiring timetable, you may be the only person running the business and doing all the necessary tasks to start, operate, and market your business. Google translator can only get you so far, and it's a good business practice to be realistic about the challenges not speaking English may present.

76. Can you obtain professional licenses to operate your business?

JC: Contact your state licensing office, easily found via search engine, to see if you or any of your employees will need a license to practice your profession.

RC: Your immigration status (or lack thereof) may have an impact on your ability to obtain the necessary licenses to operate your business. This step should be explored in the earliest planning stages, as soon as you decide what kind of vision you have and what kind of business you want to pursue. Deciding on a business you cannot legally operate is not practical. In order to be successful in your business and visa application, your business has to be viable. Do your due diligence early on.

Renata Castro, Esq., James Chittenden

77. What kind of software will you need to start your business?

JC: Write down industry-specific software your business will need, along with office or other software required to operate the business properly. Think cost-effective but scalable, so that the platform can grow with your business. Customer Relationship Management (CRM) Software, Accounting & Bookkeeping, Social Media Management, and even basic services such as Microsoft Office should be considered in addition to the industry-specific software you may adopt.

78. What kind of hardware will you need to start your business?

JC: Obviously this varies by industry, but you will need tools and equipment. Consider what you need, and how much it costs. This page is a good place to start the shopping list for tools and equipment.

Renata Castro, Esq., James Chittenden

79. Which kind of telephone service will you need to operate your business?

JC: For some smaller businesses, a simple call-forwarding service to your mobile phone is sufficient. Others require several lines and routing service. One Click Advisor (see Operate Your Business) offers solutions.

80. Do you have a system to collect, organize, and capitalize on your customers' information?

JC: The better you can make use of information about current or past customers, the better your chances of upselling and earning repeat business. A CRM (Customer Relationship Management system) offers capabilities to store customer information securely, while also providing insights on customer buying patterns that emerge over time. This enables you to further refine your marketing efforts.

Renata Castro, Esq., James Chittenden

81. Will you need credit to run your business?

JC: Think of ways to get a loan without using a U.S.-based bank. Loans are very difficult to get for businesses with less than two years of operating history, and even more difficult for non-U.S. borrowers.

82. Will your immigration status allow you to obtain credit to run your business?

RC: The U.S. government does not impose limitations on the kind of visa you need to obtain a loan, however, the less permanent your visa is, the less likely you are to obtain credit. Therefore, do your due diligence on the kind of immigration status your bank requires to issue a loan, if you will be pursuing one. This is particularly troublesome for those who enter the U.S. to explore business opportunities on a B1/B2 (nonimmigrant tourist/business) visa, and end up facing the harsh reality that it is virtually impossible to obtain credit without a social security number and a credit score. Research into this matter will save you time, money, and headaches.

83. How much capital do you need to allocate for marketing your business?

JC: A general guideline is 20% of sales should be your marketing budget. Some industries are less, and some are more.

84. Which ways can you promote your business without investing capital?

JC: You have some marketing skills at your disposal. Do all that you can for free, especially if you are in a season where money is more scarce than time. Obviously social media is free. It costs nothing to contact reporters and pitch them. See One Click Advisor (Market Your Business). You will also find a wealth of information on how to use media to promote your business in my other book, *The Public Triumph*. Get your copy for free, only cover the cost of shipping and handling IF you use the QR code and offer in this book.

Renata Castro, Esq., James Chittenden

85. Will you need to extend credit to your customers? If so, for how long?

JC: Spell out your credit terms: not too loose and not too tight. If you are extending payment terms, ensure they are not longer than terms that your suppliers have extended you.

86. What happens to your family's immigration status if your business fails?

RC: Until you obtain a green card, visas to dependents are issued in connection to the status of the main investor. Therefore, the failure of the business could mean the loss of any visa status attached to the status of the main visa applicant or investor. This is true for E-2s, International Entrepreneur Parole Rule, and O visas, for example.

Renata Castro, Esq., James Chittenden

87. Do you need to be physically present in the U.S. to start your business?

RC: Starting a business in the U.S. can present quite a quandary, as the government wants you to have taken *substantial steps* in the development of your enterprise **before** you obtain any kind of immigration benefit. A B1/B2 visa allows you to explore investment opportunities, and incorporate, but does not allow you to engage in the day-to-day activities of the enterprise. Make sure you discuss hiring timetables with your immigration attorney and budget accordingly.

88. Who will be your top three competitors?

JC: List three competitors and analyze their strengths and weaknesses, as well as opportunities and threats they face from other competitors or the economy.

Renata Castro, Esq., James Chittenden

89. If you don't have competitors, why is there no competition in your industry?

JC: A lack of competition may be a warning that the proposed business is not feasible.

RC: The açaí berry is a great illustration of this principle. Açaí in Brazil is a national passion, but the açai we eat in Brazil is *very* different from the way it is consumed in the U.S. We prepare it in a thick paste with all the add-ons you can imagine, from the healthy bowls with banana and chia seeds, to the all-out fat-fest with sweetened condensed milk and chocolate.

The açaí berry market in the U.S. is worth $720 million, so it is safe to say people in America like açai. A lot. However, every two months my office gets a call from an entrepreneur who is adamant about "showing America what really good açai tastes like." What usually happens next is that this entrepreneur opens a business that is limited to consumption by Brazilians, who are already familiar with the different textures and serving of acai, contrary to our advice. Even though the number of Brazilians in the U.S. grows tenfold every year, it is a basic business principle that the broader the audience your product appeals to, the higher your chances of success.

Think outside the box and don't rely on personal assumptions. Do your due diligence. Hire a market research company. Use services like BizMiner or other data collection and analysis services before choosing to undertake a business that is doomed to fail.

90. What kind of professional advice will you need and from whom?

JC: Have a list of professionals you will need in the day-to-day operation of your business. Running a business is quite a task, let alone running a new business in a new country. Your choice of professional advisors can make or break your business.

Bankers can be an excellent source of free advice. They know what is necessary to help you get a business loan, which is an excellent and reliable indicator of what is needed to grow and profit.

Oftentimes I witness foreign entrepreneurs lose valuable time and money by relying on the improper advice of so-called consultants. If you need immigration help, seek an immigration *lawyer*.

RC: It is not uncommon for foreigners to fall prey to unscrupulous "consultants" who practice law without a license and jeopardize your American Dream. Immigration forms have the force of law and even though filling out forms can be done by anyone, competent legal advice can only come from a lawyer. You can check your lawyer's bar license online, at no cost, for any state in which he or she is licensed. Hiring a licensed professional attorney is the smart way to protect your future.

Renata Castro, Esq., James Chittenden

91. What are your biggest fears about being an entrepreneur in the U.S.?

RC: Everyone is scared and hopeful at the beginning of their entrepreneurial journey. We have all been there and understand the fear of failure. But what does failure mean to you? Losing the money? Having to leave the U.S.? Quitting your job abroad? Once you have identified your biggest fears, you can work on reducing the likelihood that they will happen.

92. Do you have a mentor who can help you in your entrepreneurial journey?

JC: Write down the members of your "brain trust" of advisors and mentors. One piece of advice. Mentors are far more valuable than cheerleaders. Someone who picks apart your plan with constructive criticism and perhaps even hurts your feelings may do you a far greater service than a friend who simply validates your feelings while you fail.

RC: Oh, boy. I could write a whole book on this matter alone. I believe this is how many foreign entrepreneurs go down a rabbit hole that leads them to the failure of their business. When moving to a new country – and even those with money and previous experience fall prey to this trap — it is easy to feel comfortable relying on the advice of friends and family who already live in the U.S.

But that rarely proves to be fruitful, unless your friends and family are established professionals in the area in which you need advice. Seek experienced professionals. Go out of your comfort zone. How many tales of failed businesses have I heard in my years in immigration practice because the foreign investor chose to discuss the business endeavor with a friend/girlfriend/neighbor instead of obtaining the kind of advice their business endeavor (and hard earned money invested in the business) deserved? Now is not the time to be cheap nor shy.

Renata Castro, Esq., James Chittenden

93. Who will handle your payroll services?

JC: For smaller businesses in the U.S., options for payroll services are numerous, inexpensive, and accurate.

RC: Payroll records will be essential in the renewal of your immigration benefit. Having your payroll house in order from the onset will save you (and your immigration attorney) much time and hassle. Some companies prefer to have their own accountants or CPAs handle their payroll. For immigration purposes, either option works as long as your payroll records are accurate.

94. If leasing office space, will you require the assistance of a real estate broker?

JC: In the U.S., commercial real estate agents are normally paid via commission. They are paid only when a sale or lease occurs. Remember that you are entering a new country, with new customs and a new way to do business. Having the right counselors can make or break your new endeavor. Your real estate agent is no different. You can find a list of real estate agents in your area by visiting

www.nar.realtor.

95. If leasing office space, will your landlord require additional deposits or other safeguards due to your immigration status?

RC: The challenge with many of the visas designed by the U.S. government to help foreign entrepreneurs start and operate their business in the U.S., comes from the fact that the U.S. government does not consider business realities when designing these visas. Many times, if not all the time, foreign entrepreneurs must take *substantial steps* in the formation, operation, and development of their U.S.-based business even *before* a visa is considered.

This becomes particularly problematic because you will likely need a Social Security Number (SSN) in order to establish/obtain credit, and you will only get one once your case is either pending (when it comes to green cards) or when your case is approved (when it comes to non-immigrant visas).

Therefore, before falling in love with a commercial location, have your real estate agent (yes, you should have one) discuss the deposit, credit, and citizenship requirements for lease *before* you visit a location.

96. Will you need a loan to finance your business?

JC: Loans are one of many ways to finance a business. Consider others, such as equity investment capital, selling receivables, and others.

Note that conventional bank loans can be difficult to get for startup businesses in the U.S., even if the applicant is a U.S. citizen with good personal credit. Consider other sources of financing.

RC: The U.S. government is not fond of loans as seed capital for a business attached to a visa application. Before you discuss loan options with your banker, or on www.oneclickadvisor.com, make sure to speak to your immigration attorney to address any investment requirements for the kind of visa you wish to obtain for you and your family.

97. If you will need a loan, are the loan terms compliant with immigration requirements?

RC: Immigration tends to impose limits on loans, even those for businesses, if the proceeds from the loan are used to qualify for a visa, such as an E visa, for example. The U.S. government wants to know (like most banks) that you have "skin in the game" – in other words, that you stand to lose something, which would likely make you more inclined to hustle and succeed.

Not all loans are created equally. If you are taking a loan that is collateralized, that is, secured by a collateral you already own, such as a mortgage on a property, that is an acceptable source of capital. The key takeaway here is to *not* take out a loan until you have discussed the visa for which you qualify and intend to pursue with your immigration attorney.

98. Are you familiar with grants? Do you qualify for any grants?

JC: Grants awarded to for-profit businesses are very rarely direct payments to businesses or their owners. I highly recommend against incorporating grants into your plans to finance a business. Grants usually come in the form of free technical assistance to owners of businesses and start-ups. Free technical assistance IS widely available for immigrants and citizens alike. Occasionally, U.S. government grants can be awarded for small businesses that are engaged in vital scientific, technological, or medical research. Other organizations may award grants too. Grants always have highly specific qualifications.

RC: Immigration laws do not prohibit visa applicants from receiving grants; however, organizations issuing the grants set forth the requirements in order for a business to receive it. In most instances, grant money is *not* counted toward the investment amount required to obtain an immigration benefit *unless* the grant money has already been disbursed to the proposed enterprise.

Renata Castro, Esq., James Chittenden

99. What's your why?

JC: See question #1. The answer holds many clues. Take note of all that you have accomplished by answering these 99 questions and write down what very basic human needs you will solve with this business.

RC: Although being a lawyer was not a part of my childhood dreams - I wanted to be a diplomat - becoming a lawyer changed my life in more ways than one. First, I get to use my skills to give people like you, the reader of this book, effective tools to make your American dream of living, studying, investing, working and succeeding in the United States a reality. I work insane hours, travel frequently for cases all over the country, and yet, it never gets old. Being able to tell an individual that his or her case has been approved makes all the sacrifices worthwhile.

You have the answers. What now?

These 99 questions have made you think and made you research. You have your business idea. In fact, you likely have more than one. Choose the one that is most feasible.

Perhaps you are not a citizen of the U.S. and are looking to become a citizen using one of several entrepreneurship pathways. You now have identified one that may work for you.

What comes next is relatively simple. After the business has been started and registered (as a corporation, LLC, etc.), your challenges and opportunities can be sorted into one of three places.

1. **Marketing**, because marketing brings in the customers.
2. **Operations**, because a well-operated business pleases customers and provides stability.
3. **Finance**, because it keeps you paid and serves as your scoreboard.

Renata Castro, Esq., James Chittenden

It is easy to misdiagnose a problem.

For example, one entrepreneur I worked with had bought a locksmith franchise that came with an exclusive territory. His first instinct was to pursue large corporate clients and retailers. One day, a manager of a large department store chain (you've probably shopped there but they shall remain nameless here) called this locksmith with a crisis at approximately 8:30 am in the morning. The keys were lost and the store was due to open at 9 am that day.

The locksmith showed up quickly, fixed the lock, and the store opened on time. The manager was very appreciative and asked him to send his invoice to her at the store.

He sent her the invoice, and she sent it to the corporate accounts payable department. After three weeks, they noticed that this locksmith was not on their approved vendor list and sent him paperwork to complete a background check and full vetting so that he could join the approved vendor list. He completed the paperwork, and two weeks later, the auditors noticed a few errors and the human resources specialists had follow-up questions, and the company returned the paperwork to him for correction.

He was a new business owner trying to get traction. Meanwhile, this corporation was kicking him around regarding compliance with their policies and procedures, while still not paying him after several weeks. During this time, he was depleting his family's savings in an effort to keep his new business afloat.

Our advice to him was simple. First, get paid when you render the service, or don't do it. Let the department store remain locked next time if they won't pay on the spot. Second, start looking for prospects who may not be Fortune 500 companies, but are still solid customers.

We provided him a list of all strip mall owners, apartment complexes, office park managers, commercial landlords, churches, and private schools within his territory. We helped him write literature introducing himself, and helped him plan and schedule an introduction tour where he would personally visit each business.

He executed on these recommendations and the results were tremendous. He maintains good relationships and steady business throughout his territory, is adding employees, and making a good living.

As a novice business owner, he thought his inability to collect from his slow-paying and bureaucratic corporate customer was a finance problem. In reality, he just needed better customers. That is a marketing problem.

It is easy to see how making improvements in one area creates issues in other areas. For example, a business may offer credit to customers, but maintain strict credit standards. In practice, that might include refusing to sell to customers with imperfect credit histories. It might include aggressive collection efforts. This will affect revenue since you have fewer customers who can qualify to buy from you. Tight credit policies work against your marketing efforts.

On the other hand, credit policies that are too loose result in delinquent revenue for you, which results in cash flow problems. Difficulty in collecting receivables also impacts your ability to get loans from banks. All of this restricts your ability to operate property.

Expect constant trial-and-error as you look for the right combination of price, product, promotion, and place (the famous "4 P's of marketing"). All of this is subject to constant change. But you knew that already.

Renata Castro, Esq., James Chittenden

This book didn't teach you much that was new. Instead, it simply reminded you, because the knowledge was always yours.

By answering the 99 questions, you now have clarity that wasn't there before.

RECOMMENDED READING LIST

The Alchemist by **Paulo Coelho**
The 5 AM Club by **Robin Sharma**
The 4-Hour Workweek by **Timothy Ferris**
The Public Triumph by **James Chittenden**
The E-Myth by **Michael E. Gerber**
High Performance Habits by **Brendon Burchard**
Magnetic Marketing by **Dan Kennedy**
The Four Agreements by **Don Miguel Ruiz**
The Millions Within by **David Neagle**
Think and Grow Rich by **Napoleon Hill**
How to Read a Financial Report by **John A. Tracy**
How to Win Friends and Influence People by **Dale Carnegie**
The Seven Habits of Highly Effective People by **Stephen Covey**
Play Bigger by **Al Ramadan**
Atomic Habits by **James Clear**
Rich Dad's Cashflow Quadrant by **Robert Kiyosaki**
Rich Dad Poor Dad by **Robert Kiyosaki**

ABOUT THE AUTHORS

Renata Castro, Esq is an award-winning immigration attorney and founder of (https://castrolegalgroup.com), a national immigration practice based out of Coral Springs, Florida. A frequent fixture on TV and radio shows, Renata has spoken on the issue of immigration law and policy for outlets such as CNN Brasil, CBS12, Fox5, Black News Channel, to name a few.

An avid traveler, Renata's happy place is in the Appalachian Mountains of Georgia, where she enjoys the views of blueberry fields in the back of her lodge in Clayton.

James Chittenden is a celebrated business consultant and founder of One Click Advisor, a centralized hub for those seeking to start, market, finance, or operate their businesses. He has guided thousands of business owners and aspiring entrepreneurs on the path of building a solid and profitable business.

This is the second published book James has authored, along with dozens of articles and digital downloads providing advice on small business challenges. He's an accomplished public speaker who has been featured on all major television networks.

He has written articles for *Forbes*, the *Houston Chronicle*, and *Preferred Magazine*.

James is a former U.S. Marine Corps officer, who parlayed the duress of military training and service into business resilience and success. He's also an amateur boxing champion, who serves part-time as a professional boxing and MMA (mixed martial arts) official.

ABOUT THE EDITOR

Sarah Rumpf currently serves as the Contributing Editor at *Mediaite*. Her writing has been featured at *National Review*, *The Daily Beast*, *Reason*, *Independent Journal Review*, *Law & Crime*, *Texas Monthly*, *The Capitolist*, *The Orlando Sentinel*, the *Austin-American Statesman*, and numerous other media outlets and websites. She's been ranked on the best political Twitter lists in three states (Florida, Massachusetts, and Texas), and her political commentary has led to appearances on the BBC, MSNBC, Fox News, Fox 35 Orlando, Fox 7 Austin, and other television, radio, and podcast programs across the globe.

A native Floridian, Sarah attended the University of Florida, including a summer abroad at the *Universität Mannheim* in Mannheim, Germany, graduating with a double major in Political Science and German. She graduated with her Juris Doctor, *cum laude*, from UF's College of Law and practiced in Orlando for several years before launching her own campaign consulting and strategic communications company. She has advised a long list of political party organizations, PACs, nonprofits, think tanks, businesses, and local, state, and federal campaigns on election and campaign finance law, communications strategies, social media, public relations, and grassroots outreach.